ALL ABOUT ARACHNIDS
TARANTULAS

by Becca Becker

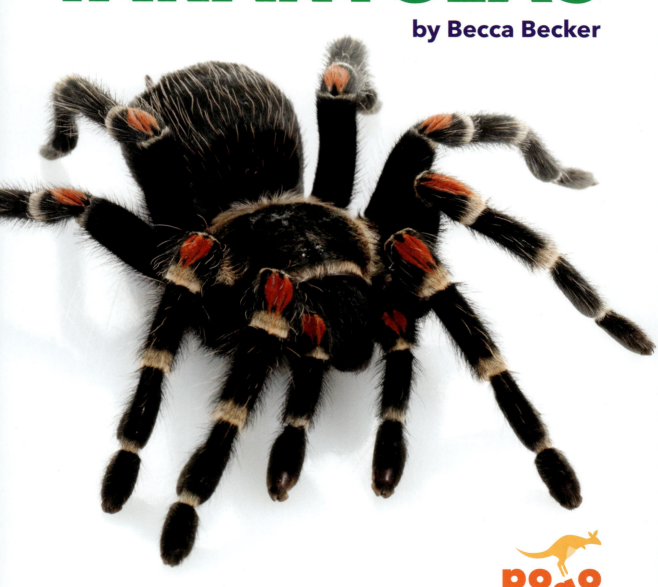

pogo

Ideas for Parents and Teachers

Pogo Books let children practice reading informational text while introducing them to nonfiction features such as headings, labels, sidebars, maps, and diagrams, as well as a table of contents, glossary, and index.

Carefully leveled text with a strong photo match offers early fluent readers the support they need to succeed.

Before Reading

- "Walk" through the book and point out the various nonfiction features. Ask the student what purpose each feature serves.
- Look at the glossary together. Read and discuss the words.

Read the Book

- Have the child read the book independently.
- Invite them to list questions that arise from reading.

After Reading

- Discuss the child's questions. Talk about how they might find answers to those questions.
- Prompt the child to think more. Ask: What did you know about tarantulas before reading this book? What more would you like to learn about them?

Pogo Books are published by Jump!
5357 Penn Avenue South
Minneapolis, MN 55419
www.jumplibrary.com

Copyright © 2025 Jump! International copyright reserved in all countries. No part of this book may be reproduced in any form without written permission from the publisher.

Library of Congress Cataloging-in-Publication Data

Names: Becker, Becca, author.
Title: Tarantulas / by Becca Becker.
Description: Minneapolis, MN: Jump!, Inc., [2025]
Series: All about arachnids | Includes index.
Audience: Ages 7-10
Identifiers: LCCN 2024032970 (print)
LCCN 2024032971 (ebook)
ISBN 9798892136211 (hardcover)
ISBN 9798892136228 (paperback)
ISBN 9798892136235 (ebook)
Subjects: LCSH: Tarantulas—Juvenile literature.
Classification: LCC QL458.42.T5 B428 2025 (print)
LCC QL458.42.T5 (ebook)
DDC 595.4/4—dc23/eng/20240830
LC record available at https://lccn.loc.gov/2024032970
LC ebook record available at https://lccn.loc.gov/2024032971

Editor: Katie Chanez
Designer: Emma Almgren-Bersie

Photo Credits: pick-uppath/iStock, cover; Natalie Ruffing/iStock, 1; GlobalP/iStock, 3; Kurit afshen/Shutterstock, 4; duckycards/iStock, 5; monster_code/Shutterstock, 6-7; Tracy Wesolek/iStock, 8-9tl; Parkerspics/Shutterstock, 8-9tr; Uwe-Bergwitz/iStock, 8-9bl; blickwinkel/Alamy, 8-9br; Close to Me Photography/Shutterstock, 10-11; Tobias Hauke/Shutterstock, 12; Ryan M. Bolton/Shutterstock, 13, 18-19; ConstantinCornel/iStock, 14-15; Ben Gingell/Shutterstock, 16; John Mitchell/Science Source, 17; Audrey Snider-Bell/Shutterstock, 20-21; dwi putra stock/Shutterstock, 23.

Printed in the United States of America at Corporate Graphics in North Mankato, Minnesota.

TABLE OF CONTENTS

CHAPTER 1
Big and Hairy...4

CHAPTER 2
Mating and Molting.......................................12

CHAPTER 3
Predator and Prey...16

ACTIVITIES & TOOLS
Try This!..22
Glossary..23
Index...24
To Learn More..24

CHAPTER 1
BIG AND HAIRY

An **arachnid** crawls. Its eight legs are covered in hair. So is its large body. What is this spider? It is a tarantula!

Tarantulas live on every continent but Antarctica. They like warm areas, such as rain forests, deserts, and **scrublands**.

CHAPTER 1 | 5

CHAPTER 1

Some tarantulas live under logs and stones. Some live in trees. Others live in **burrows**.

Tarantulas make silk webs. But the webs are not for catching **prey**. A tarantula spins a web in its home. The web keeps dirt and sand out.

DID YOU KNOW?

A tarantula might have a line of silk that goes to the burrow entrance. Why? If an animal touches it, the silk moves. The tarantula knows an animal is close.

CHAPTER 1 | 7

There are around 900 tarantula **species**. Each looks different. The desert tarantula is tan. Why? It blends in with sand. The pink-toed tarantula has pink on the tips of its legs.

The Brazilian salmon pink birdeater is one of the largest tarantulas. It weighs as much as a banana. The Trinidad dwarf tarantula is small. It is as long as two paper clips!

desert tarantula

pink-toed tarantula

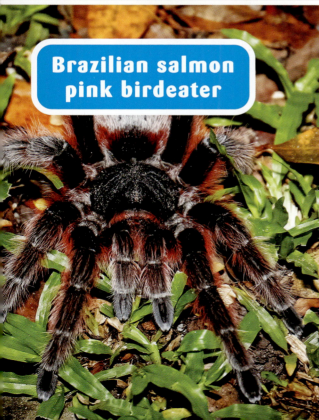
Brazilian salmon pink birdeater

Trinidad dwarf tarantula

All tarantulas have the same body parts. They use pedipalps to feel. These also help hold prey.

pedipalps

CHAPTER 1

TAKE A LOOK!

What are the parts of a tarantula? Take a look!

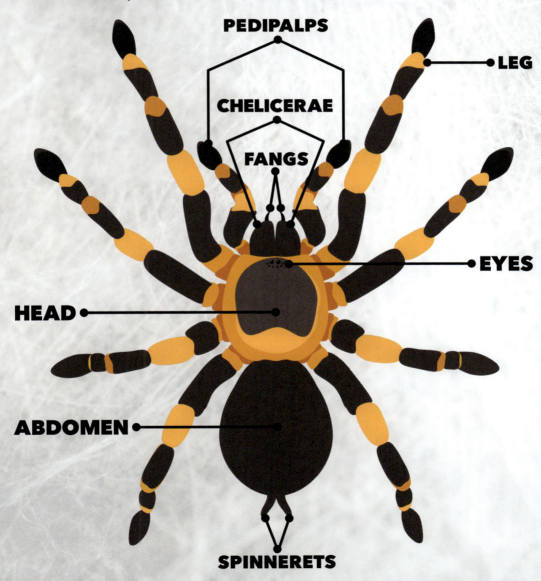

CHAPTER 1 · 11

CHAPTER 2
MATING AND MOLTING

Adult tarantulas **mate**. Some females eat the male after! Why? The **nutrients** help her lay eggs. She wraps her eggs in an egg sac. She guards it.

egg sac

After six to nine weeks, hundreds of **spiderlings** come out of the egg sac. They stay with mom for two to three weeks. Then they live on their own.

spiderlings

CHAPTER 2

Every tarantula has an exoskeleton. This is a hard outer casing on its body. A tarantula sheds its exoskeleton many times as it grows. Why? Its body gets too big for the old one. This is called molting.

CHAPTER 2

CHAPTER 3
PREDATOR AND PREY

Tarantulas are skilled **predators**. They hunt at night. They catch **insects**, mice, and frogs. How? They wait for prey to come close. Then they grab it with their legs!

The goliath bird spider eats birds, too. It is the largest tarantula in the world. It is as big as a dinner plate!

After it catches prey, the tarantula bites it. Its fangs have **venom**. The prey cannot move. Its insides turn to liquid. The tarantula sucks it up. Yum!

DID YOU KNOW?

Tarantula bites can be painful! But their venom does not kill humans.

CHAPTER 3 | 19

Animals like coyotes and snakes eat tarantulas. Tarantulas protect themselves. Some lift their front legs to look bigger. They show their fangs. They look scary! Others have special hairs on their abdomens. They kick the hairs off. These hurt the predator's eyes and nose.

Tarantulas only attack when they are scared. They would rather leave people alone. Would you like to see one?

DID YOU KNOW?

A predator might rip off a tarantula's leg. But the tarantula can regrow it when it molts.

20 CHAPTER 3

CHAPTER 3

ACTIVITIES & TOOLS

TRY THIS!

PIPE CLEANER TARANTULA

Make a tarantula with this fun activity!

What You Need:
- 1 soda can tab
- 4 black pipe cleaners
- 4 brown pipe cleaners
- scissors

1. Cut your pipe cleaners in half.
2. Twist one black and one brown pipe cleaner together. Do this with the rest until you have eight pieces.
3. Twist the eight pieces onto the soda can tab.
4. Bend the pieces. Now you have hairy tarantula legs!

GLOSSARY

arachnid: A creature with a body divided into two parts, such as a spider or a scorpion.

burrows: Tunnels or holes in the ground used as animal homes.

insects: Small animals with three pairs of legs, one or two pairs of wings, and three main body parts.

mate: To come together to produce babies.

nutrients: Substances that animals need to stay strong and healthy.

predators: Animals that hunt other animals for food.

prey: Animals hunted by other animals for food.

scrublands: Areas covered with stunted trees or shrubs.

species: One of the groups into which similar animals and plants are divided.

spiderlings: Baby spiders.

venom: Poison.

INDEX

Brazilian salmon pink birdeater 8
burrows 7
deserts 5
desert tarantula 8
eggs 12
egg sac 12, 13
exoskeleton 15
fangs 11, 19, 20
goliath bird spider 17
hair 4, 20
insects 16
mate 12

molting 15, 20
nutrients 12
pedipalps 10, 11
pink-toed tarantula 8
predators 16, 20
prey 7, 10, 16, 19
rain forests 5
scrublands 5
species 8
spiderlings 13
Trinidad dwarf tarantula 8
webs 7

TO LEARN MORE

Finding more information is as easy as 1, 2, 3.

❶ Go to www.factsurfer.com
❷ Enter "tarantulas" into the search box.
❸ Choose your book to see a list of websites.

ACTIVITIES & TOOLS